Picking Weeds and Calling Them Flowers

Picking Weeds and Calling Them Flowers

Gracie Drew

ISBN 9798218499327

for the people who are carrying silent burdens.

Content Warning

This book contains themes such as sexual abuse, neglect, self-harm, suicidal ideation, obsessive-compulsive thoughts, anxiety, depression, and other potentially triggering material. Please read with care and caution. Thank you.

Foreword

it's 1am as i sit down to type this out to you, my reader. my fairy lights are creating a yellow-like cast over me, and the screen of my laptop lights up my face and i'm embarrassed to say that i am awake for the day. i don't know how to tell you this, but i live with bipolar disorder, and these things, these nights where i am awake for too long, happen far too often. i have to say, this just happens sometimes. it's all chemical. but this collection couldn't have happened without it, and for that i am grateful. i am tired and happy and angry and more than i've ever been within the last almost twenty-three years.

this collection took up an entire therapy session yesterday and in a way is my own compilation of therapy sessions. it is all the moments i've spent being nothing but wanting to be more. it's my desperation pressed between pages, and i hope you're able to understand where i'm coming from when i say that poetry over the years has almost killed me just as much as it has almost saved me.

so, i hope you enjoy these poems that i've pieced together from when i was sixteen all the way up until present day. this is many parts of me that i'm laying out for you to find yourself in. to know you aren't alone in the suffering and the healing and the confusing twists and turns of a burdening childhood. to know there is so much more to life than bad days and tear-stained pillowcases.

the fickleness of things

being the little girl
picking weeds and calling them flowers.
giving my mother bouquets
that die overnight.
getting grass stains on my knees
and ticks on my ankles from
playing where i was told not to.
my stepfather tearing them
from my skin, leaving a dot
of blood behind.
glow sticks and lightning bugs
dancing through summer night skies.
ice pops melting down my hands
making everything sticky.
my hair entering my mouth as
the wind blows through it
while i ride my bike down the street
but only to the stop sign and back.
getting growing pains in my knees
and getting too big for my
favorite shorts.
getting car sick and being glued
to my father's side.
standing on my tip toes in the
deep end of a pool.
looking like my grandma when the sun
reflects off my bright orange hair
and showcases my freckled face.
being the little girl
picking weeds and calling them
flowers.

something to clean up

a fragile being.
a faint whisper.
the girl you see
through the bus window
as you wait to cross the street.
a smudge or nagging ball of lint
stuck to the window
disturbing the perfection of things.

i don't like what i'm writing

it's been too long since i last wrote
and it shows.
i am not proud of myself in the ways
people say i should be.
i turn twenty-two this month and i think
that's too old for me.
i don't think it suits me.
i am still a child at heart.
this is how i say that
i never let go of my mother.
or my father for that matter.
time passes and the people,
the people outside, their lives
never stopped moving.
and i'm grieving.
there is always something to
miss;
i just wish for my mother
that thing was me
but i am a tragedy before
i am alive.

the recollection of things

my arms sting just
the same.
i am a leaf in the breeze
that tells you
soon the days will
get shorter,
and you will get sadder.
the bad news.
the remembering that burns
too.

seasons

i love the in between of
summer and winter
enough to keep myself alive
to see the end of it.
the trees tell me
something has to be worth
something; not everything
is what it seems.
they mean this in the best way.
it means what my mother
made out of me
is not all i will be,
or even something
i've ever been.
it is the breeze that
keeps me steady.
pushing me forward
through the unknown
of growing up.

the skin you shed

the bittersweet taste of leaving
your childhood home behind
and all the skin you had shed
all those years
inside it
under the bed
you slept in.
writing poetry to hold onto it
for a little bit longer.
remembering your mother
picking apples and calling you
inside for dinner.
the days, they never end, even when
it's dark and the coyotes have made
themselves known in your backyard.
you are too full of youth
to fall asleep and stay in it.
maybe that part never left you.
maybe you only say goodbye
to the things that hurt you.
maybe you recall yourself
and you learn to love that part
of growing up too.

ashley

i'll spin myself around with
my hair long and tangled.
smelling of vanilla and
wanting more.
i will be a gentle thing.
i don't want to leave my mark
on this earth.
i want to be
who you miss quietly.
to be someone
you almost wish you were.

the windows are open and i am the same

my birthday is too soon.
i still feel fifteen and unready.
i am still the kid
brushing their mother's hair
and always dreaming about
something.

i am trying to grow my hair out
like i once had it.
bangs and all.
waves of orange blaze.
hoping it helps me
reconnect with something
that remains bigger than me.

i am always growing but
never changing.
never knowing better.
finding myself in
the grave
over and over again.
putting myself there
in the first place.

front porch

in atlanta, i sit on the front porch
trying not to notice the weight
in my heart from the holidays.
it is warmer here than it is
in boston.
it is sunnier.
the breeze goes by and
i think about how much
my mother would love this.
how much i wish
things were easier for us
both.
i don't know what
she's up to anymore
and it's not like i want to
but part of me feels like
i need to run and save her
from herself as i did for
all those years.
it is funny how i will always
circle back to her
even when things are going well.
she is where i go to remind myself
i will always be a little bit
of nothing.

busy street

i try to write in the sun
and imagine myself as a kid again,
only i've forgotten most
of this story.
playing reels in my head
of my bangs getting in my eyes
and my father pushing me
on my bike.
there are so many ways
to tell it like it is.
there are so many ways i could be
but am not.
i try to piece together the parts
i remember.
softening the edges of
memory.
i try to write in the sun
and nothing pulls out of me
but grief.

cold hands

it gets colder everyday
and it's even worse
at night.
the sun is setting at 6pm
and i hate it more than i despise
my own hands for
becoming too stiff
to uncover myself from
the blanket that i swear protects me
from the big bad things
that don't exist anymore.

must

in all those days and many hours
i spent cowering over myself
from behind my own body,
i died deaths one after the other.

i am asked if i want to die, and to this,
i have to say no.
instead i spit out the truth; i want to live
and this is why i must die.
the devastation that follows the
warm day in the middle of winter,
the one that knocks you off your feet
and into a pit of childhood memories.

yearning is asking to be let down.
sickness of the brain means
nothing is what it is.
there is always the one thing we want
but can't have.

i miss my childhood home.
it should've been good to me.
it wasn't, but it should've been.

i don't have any thoughts of suicide

i need to keep myself alive
long enough to see
if it gets better.
if my mother finally apologizes.
if my medications start to work better.
if my body stops hurting from the moment i wake up.

i need to keep myself alive long enough
to see myself matter.
to see my brother again.
to see city skylines that make me
want to break out of my shell
and try.

i need to keep myself alive long enough
to feel the feeling of wanting to live.
to feel the relief of a deep breath.
to feel the sensation across my skin
the chlorine filled pool water makes
as i shoot up through it.
to feel like it wasn't my fault.

florida

i remember the times
i walked to the park
in the last town i lived in,
the really small and ugly one
and wanted to kill myself
in the surrounding woods.
it was always rainy
and me, sneaking out of the
fence gate, trying not to
let the metal shriek.
it was so persistent,
the wanting to die.
it was unlike my mother
in that way.

it was so easy to
slip out of my body
and think about what i could
do to it as a bystander to my
own skin.
it was so vile at fourteen.
the last time i hurt myself
was roughly age fifteen.

i remember the feeling
of sitting on the bench
and feeling the waves
of nothing and everything
in a cyclical way.
i sunk under the depths of
the florida humidity.
slipping in and out
of wanting to fight.

i would make my way home
after staring down
my own hands and feeling
so far away for at least an hour
and i knew i'd never say a thing.

shell bay

i eat port wine cheese
that i bought from a local
farmers market on a day that
is warmer than the last
but could be better.
i start to miss my father
in between the beats
of my heart.
my body is a vessel
i have not yet forgiven.
the memories of
a jersey campfire with
cheddar chips and my dad's
hand wrapped around
a bud light
bounce around my head
and i try not to get stuck
in what he could've been.
he comes and goes
like a breeze i feel
on these days.
taking my breath away
but allowing me to feel
all at once.
without the moments of
missing him, i don't know
i'd exist. i don't know
that i'd be all that human.
wanting is twisted within
my anatomy and i can
cry in the shower or buy cheese
everyday
but i will always end up
back in this place.

a lost daughter

a porch swing has been
my childhood dream
for as long as i can remember.
i think it is ultimately peace
that i want.
maybe i am trying to recreate
a version of the story
where my father pulls up
in his pick-up truck, the one
i was devastated over
when he trashed it,
and loves me enough
to look me in the eye
even when i am covered
in the mud i was told
not to touch.
even when i am angry
and yelling and gnawing
at my hair like it'll
make the realization
of our relationship
dissolving into
nothing not hurt
as much as it does.

the leaves are changing

the fall has dripped into
my life and it's colder
than i remember.
there are so many things
that have lived
and never left a mark
on this earth
and i worry i will
fade the same.
if you feel anything,
i want it to be the things
i have felt
when the wind blows
softly
through the weeds
and dying leaves.
or the days i have gotten
out of bed with a glimmer
in my chest that i believed
was a second sun
convincing me there is
something good left
just for me.

generations

i swallowed the fire that is being
the first-born daughter and watched as it
did to me what it did to my mother.
maybe it's about my father;
his coldness, the toughness he wants to wear
like it's really there.
i am resentfully more him
than i am me sometimes i think
and this hurts bigger than my body.
i want to have something of my own,
something that can soften the edges
of my adolescence and make it into something
worth remembering how to write for.

i wouldn't say i'm in denial but i don't know what else to call it

i text my therapist almost regularly
and she tells me that she's happy that i want to save myself.
i tell her i wouldn't be here if
my parents loved me more than
they're ashamed of themselves
and i'm told that eventually it starts with you
and what you
aren't willing to do
(i hate this more than my father but it doesn't matter).
i go on and teach myself about cycles
in between our sessions,
about how mother usually hates daughter
when daughter is too much like mother
and how father just does not know any better
and i will leave this gutted part of me alone.

i start to resent that some of my mothers
sob stories are real.
that somewhere in my heart i will always be
begging for her
with a little voice that's almost like a ringing in your ear.
there's pieces of wanting in me that i see like
a weakness and they do, they weaken me.

i realize the nightmares won't stop until i peel away at
my childhood like a scab that just won't stop itching,

she tells me it's important to process,
to stop gliding my tongue across my uneven teeth
and being surprised when it's sore.
but how could i look at it for what it is and let it go
like it's nothing? i couldn't.

but i never know where to start when i pick up the phone
and she asks if i'd like to talk about my childhood,
so, i tell her
it's not really something i want to talk about because
i'm over it, i am.
and i go on stomaching it, somehow.

try and tell me

try and tell me
that you aren't avoiding all the corners
of your childhood because there is no
easy way to talk about it.
because saying you can talk about your mother
without thinking about how some things
just don't work out
and that you can think about sex
without the intrusion and sinking feeling
of not being ready
doesn't only make you feel ashamed
but dishonest.

some holes never close

it starts with a house,
one you're supposed
to know forever,
which you thankfully take no part in,
or at least try not to.
the neighbors star in this idea of forever,
the one you've always dreamt of
but never had because sometimes people
just don't get what they want
so they end up becoming escape routes,
who you go to when your phone line has been disconnected,
when your life is in danger by a man
who simply isn't there
and you're not sure if he's left
or if he was never there to begin with.

there's a soulmate down the street,
well, it's elementary school, so it's more of a crush
but you don't know the difference,
at seventeen, he's a bully
and you still don't know the difference.

it will be hard to admit that people can go on without loving you.
swirl the disappointment around and spit it out
but remember it will always find a way to come back,
it will just look different every time,
sometimes like your mother and sometimes yourself.
think about home and try not to scream,
at least not until you can handle admitting
that you're not sure if it's forever
but you always knew it was
going to leave a mark.

cyclical

you are earth shattering but don't know much else.
you are nothing short of a void after that
and even though it's so regular,
you are scared that it will never end, that this time
you are not strong enough to handle being alone.
you are sick of damage control and
apologizing for things
you are always going to say again.
you are sure this is it, that this is the sum of you
and everything you've done.
you are so unsure if it's worth it in the end.
you are so willing yet
you are tired.

playing cards with almost parents

i tie rocks to my ankles. i believe it should be moral to give up, or
at the very least, acceptable.
but you wouldn't believe the misunderstandings mothers
and their mothers
have about holes and the way they consume everything
yet become nothing in the end.
how tsunamis are just waves with grief to release
and gods to go against.
how it's painful to be the destruction and to see what you reek
because of it. how they make it about them again and again but in
all the wrong ways.
how you are seventeen and want to be a miracle, nothing short of
something worth mentioning, of loving
(in the worst case—or most cases—or my case).

college? / i don't need it / you need everything.

there's storms my mother is afraid of, that i welcome, this is our
difference.
she is running around in circles, never building a home and never
thinking about it and i am begging for the soil to let me sink in,
stay put, and put a life together that sticks.
with the selfishness crawling in through her ears, always years
behind me, always looking me in the eye
(or through me),
lecturing me on the importance of listening to what is not being
said, reading between the lines,
noticing where the empathy ends and
the disappointment starts
(it's always in a sundress, even in winter).
her molecules make up half of mine,
as do my fathers.
their failures are statues to study and avoid at all costs.
don't bring them up
but don't forget that they're there
(so nothing like them, not at all).

our mothers and their mothers believe they know
about the end of the world, they think about being let
down and they think of us,
or they don't
(they both mean the same thing).

but my mother does not lick my wounds and my
father
does not admit
where they came from
and i'm the only one who knows shame

(with an upbringing like that?)
(how could i not?)

close the blinds

home alone, the anxiety makes a fool out of me
as i try so desperately to slow my heart and fall asleep;
watching how it doesn't work.
i have to leave the house tonight and knowing this
makes a bad day out of a thursday that could've
been better because it's almost friday.
i write watching a skyline so beautiful and broad
that it makes me crave getting better.
i want to walk up and down each street and make friends
with a stranger and not think much more about
what could come next.
fall is approaching and i want to be okay by then,
to be able to think about outside without
tensing up and sending my boyfriend on his way
to do the things i should be able to.

remembering

i listen to music that helps me want to die;
this is not a good feeling but it isn't new either.
it feels so scary getting old and i cry until my head
pounds right between my eyebrows, begging me
to do something about the sadness. i hear cries
for help and even make my own. i get back in bed
and nothing gets done because even if i do everything,
there's this insatiable want to do more, to be more,
and criticism becomes my motivation. maybe it's
turning into something ugly but how do i tell myself
that it will be okay? that i will not always need to call
my mother and vent about how i've been so sick for
so long? i up my meds and wait for something new.
this is brutal. my stomach turns and i cry over
the grief left in my chest from my father never
calling back, from never calling in the first place.
my psychiatrist asks who has hurt me and i confide,
regretfully. this will have consequences later.

dead girl walking

there are leaves in my mouth and dirt under my nails.
no one notices i'm gone because there is no one left.
there is no missing persons and i think he loves me. i wish there was
more to the story than a father and daughter, but you already know the
rest. blood drips from my nose and the taste of metal is not anything
if not familiar. this is a home. this is where i die and keep missing him.
i know men's eyes like the back of my right hand. i know control, the
sense of ownership over a woman. i know what a man that size could do
to a girl.

sex and the city
after Olivia Gatwood

i want to write at a desk in front of a window
overlooking the city i love and i'm not afraid
of being alone
in my shoebox apartment that i hate
but love the same.
writing poetry i will be scared of.
oh, what i could be if i wasn't scared
of the idea of being afraid.
i wonder where it comes from.
i toss it around my mouth like a tooth
that's finally fallen out
and then i remember i've never been brave, only forced.
this does not give me the courage to survive,
only enough adrenaline to get me to where i am, and
even then, i'm dissatisfied.
the apartment is falling apart and i accept it the
same way i do my body.
oh, to be a woman who loves coffee and
doesn't end up dead
by the end of the story.
to be a woman who walks into a party,
the one no one thought would show up,
but was just happy she did.
to be so important that
you almost stopped wanting to die.

mother of god

i read that you can tell when a woman kills. i read this from a book, who read it from somewhere else, and now i'm reciting it. it made me think of my mother. you're supposed to love her, to want her when you are stranded in the depths of your depression and she's supposed to come, she's supposed to hear your cries before they leave your mouth but bleeding out was never going to be enough.

relapse

the thing you thought
would save you
doesn't in the end
and you're left to wonder
where all the blood goes.
down the sink, or the bathtub drain.
either way it's no longer
in your body
and you're the one
who made the first cut.
but you don't realize this yet.
not until it's much later
and the sun has set and you
wait for your boyfriend in
the comfort of your own bed and
try to ignore the stinging
coming from underneath
a gauze wrap that you swore
you wouldn't need again.

the walk home

the top of the trees, crisp in the heights of the yellow sky, a mother leaves her child to fend for themselves before they're ready to. you do not fall out of the nest so much as you are pushed. this is the first time you learned not to trust anything. this is where you picked up on burying yourself until no one could hear you scream had you ever built up the courage to want to live. stumble home, notice the person sleeping on the bench and how your shoulders tense up around any man who looks like he could kill you and not say a word for the rest of his life. he would even visit your grave, leave flowers and send his condolences to your aching mother. he is the good guy here. he is the good guy you let into your heart and then into your bed and then without having a say, into your body. he sickens you from the inside out, pulling at every vessel, wrapping his burley knuckles around your heart just to let you know he can. this wasn't supposed to go here. this wasn't supposed to be a story about a man who broke you, but it always goes back to this place. you are always revisiting the ways he loved you, even the ways he hated you because they were always almost the same thing.

on a tuesday afternoon i am nothing

i lay in bed with a quiet yet bringing me to my death desperation. all i can do is write about the ways i die, but this is because i'm familiar with carrying on like nothing happened, with carrying the burden of not knowing how to talk about it other than as if it's still happening. i don't care if it's getting old, i don't care if it's repetitive and not to the point enough because i'm not sleeping, still, after all these years. i'm reminiscing and it's not romantic, it's not to recall something to help keep me going. i don't go into the kitchen all day. my anxiety bounds me by my ankles and wrists, so, here i am, here i am victim again but this time to myself. this is embarrassing. if only being human was forgivable. this kind of human is resentful, it is shameful and humiliating to be scared of the very thing that will save you from your own demise. i prey on myself and devour my own body until nothing but bone is left, and even then, i keep going. i suck on what's left of my pathetic attempt to stay alive. i pick my teeth with it when i'm finished and i lay in bed with a quiet yet never ending this is it.

i am always calling it love

i am always revisiting the place you hated me
and called it love.
maybe the fighting was never going to be worth it but i thought
we were going to make it at some point.
i thought i could stomach you forever.
at least until i was sinking into my mother's bed
and crying my eyes out
because one day you were there
and the next there was nothing left.
don't kill me this time, let me do it myself.
let me admit to you that i will always love you.
this is me accepting defeat. this is me telling you
that you're where i go to eat myself alive.

all on my own

i am sat in bed on a empty tuesday morning,
rain pouring and thunder matching the rhythm
of my deprived yet somehow still full heart.
i feel calmer than i did yesterday
and maybe it's because i slept in
a little longer today
but it feels like a revelation,
like maybe i could keep myself alive
all on my own.

happiness feels like a certain kind
of boredom, because it is ease
that we really want.
i am happiest when i am messy headed,
sweating under multiple throw blankets and
on the verge of falling asleep at noon.
it doesn't come often,
though i think it should.

til' death do us part

oh, the things a woman can hide behind her teeth
when she is scared of the man she loves.
the knife under the pillow is only a whisper of the gun
in the safe just in the closet outside the bedroom.
you know this story, you know that even though this ends with
a house on fire and you halfway down the driveway with his
blood on your t-shirt and his body cold on the floor, he's not
done yet.

because i am twenty

a mother was never going to be the answer of adulthood but it
would've helped had she loved me more
when i was young.
i try to forgive her, now.
i am twenty and always going to need her
in my saddest depths,
to pick me up and weave me back together.

i am twenty and one night, back in the summer of i think 2016, she
sits me on the dock at our airbnb
and tells me she's sorry
and i tell her i know what it's like to be a woman, that i know the
story does not end with what a father knows how to do, or what he
does not.

i am twenty and there's a long line of victimization and i happened to
be old enough
but still ripe enough to get in the way of it
and of course, it had teeth,
of course, it was going to rip me apart in ways that make
it hard to sleep
but i try to forgive her because i am twenty
and i still need my mother,
now more than ever.

you made me hate this city

at this time of year, the sun is setting at 6pm and you can hear the
wind make its way through this ugly city.
i won't say i hate it, it's how i've survived, where i've made a life for
myself with someone i love and people who want to know me.
though it is scary to be in a place so much bigger than yourself,
somewhere a building, or a car, or a biker, could crush you
at any moment.
i'm both important and unimportant and i think
i like to slip between the cracks every once in a while. especially
when the nights are longer than the days.
but work has been good, there's not much to complain about other
than my feet hurt and it's getting cold.
i still miss my father, though it's quieter than it is in the summer
because we have more memories there.
this is about my city and how it's starting to become his. not my
fathers but someone almost like him.
i didn't want to hate it here, but you are

coming too close to home.

doubt

i convinced myself that my boyfriend didn't love me because he didn't frighten me and this is how i remember you.

loss

i know eventually you must
get out of bed at least once.
i don't know what to do with my heart
when it is doing the thing it does
and i don't know
what to do with my head when i am tired.
i am asking you to carry the burden of loving me
just enough, just until i can love myself
back into myself again.

movies are all gore and no depth

horror movies remind me
of my own mortality and
in some ways this
takes me back to my father.
it always comes down to
getting through what could
kill me if it tried
a little harder.

i don't know where this goes but i need to put it somewhere

i carry my bag of bones
from one place to
another
and hope something good
comes out of the way
it is raining today.
i take it as a sign
that giving up is only
right sometimes.
it is a sunday afternoon,
or barely,
and there is nothing left
but the mundane things
i think will save me.
like the smell of lavender
mixed with chamomile
or the lit candle across
the room.
i know the world keeps going
without me
and it will inevitably move on
when i am nothing
because i've been
and i am.

you bring yourself to the show and it never mattered if you came or
not

being important,
it never comes.
it is never enough
to be loved.
an insatiable hunger.
i bare my teeth
when i am sad.
keeping out the possibility
of the realization
that nothing ever mattered
even when i thought
it did.
on a stage
i am the silence
filling the room.
the awkwardness when
there is nothing left to say.
being someone who matters
comes so slow.
the wanting comes
ten fold.

a love letter to girlhood

so, maybe girlhood isn't about being broken down by men and boys who you beg to love you right and crying into your pillow because you and your mom fought again simply because you're a reflection of her. maybe it's about summer and the music that releases during that time that makes you dance around your living room in a towel after a fresh shower. because some days i sit on my floor and do my makeup in the mirror and other days i go to the park on my own and enjoy the wind while i write poetry about feeling better and it keeps me alive. it reminds me to keep myself alive and i pull myself from my grimy childhood and reclaim the girlhood i never got to have and even though it makes me sad to remember all that i missed out on, i know i can wake up and brush my hair and wear an oversized t-shirt and kiss my boyfriend and the things that happened or didn't won't matter because i do.

sugar cookies

the candle i lit
this morning
has my whole
apartment
smelling of sweet
cookies.

it takes me back
to christmas as a kid.
baking with
my family
in the clean kitchen.

my feet on a step stool
and leaning over
a crowded counter
full of flour and dough
balls.
my mother's laugh
ringing my ear
even now.

taking photos to save
the moment.
not realizing they'd
fizzle into forgotten and
unimportant traditions.

butterflies

my father used to say that i picked things up as quickly as i put them down and i'm ashamed that this is still true as a twenty-two-year-old-something trying to find who they are under broken relationships and goodbyes they didn't know were the last. something about him being right feels like my wings are being broken off and hung to display in cases on walls in old homes or to dangle from the ear of someone who loves themself and this part just makes me bitter. i'm a left out girl in a world too big to fit into their perception of normalcy and even though i wake each day with resilience, there is a part of me, or several, that wish i would stop fighting, that i would let my dad win, because navigating a body you don't like feels as though you are an embarrassment and even if i'm something to hide, i just wish he wasn't right about the ways i don't matter. i wonder if i will ever stop looking for him in corner stores and little girls with braids in their hair that their father no doubt learned how to do just to make them happy and i pick things up as quickly as i put them down because i'm trying to find him in something consistent. like looking for a ghost in your dirty home that you swear must be haunted because there's no love. none.

girlhood is

1) writing a letter to your mother
that you will never send
that is full of admissions of grief.
2) sitting on the tub floor
during a shower
and contemplating what part of you
you should change first.
3) looking like your father
but not knowing anything
past his name.
4) listening to mitski
with the window open
and hoping you're not
letting anyone down
by being sad again.
5) wanting to be someone else
but not knowing who
so you stay the same
and it hurts.
6) missing your childhood home
but writing about how
you never want to go back.
7) shedding your skin and saying
you're fine while
blood stains your sleeve.
8) needing love to feel human
and never being able to
give it to yourself.

shower

i hate how my hair
looks when it's dry
and how it feels
when it's wet.
either way,
i am never satisfied
with what i am
when the sun sets
and it's just me
at 8pm
trying to make a home
somewhere within my bed
or on my couch
and each time, i end up
on my bathroom floor
picking apart my skin and scalp
thinking something will save me
from myself and the loneliness
and that feeling in my chest
that i get when i realize
it's only me.

long island

there's something about the way
the inside of my closet smells
that reminds me of
my childhood home
back on long island.
it reminds me of
my mother's arms
and even though
we don't talk anymore
i just hope she knows
or has an inkling
that i miss her
even if she doesn't miss me back.

growing pains

i want to dance around
my apartment
in nothing but a tank top
and underwear
and feel the weight lift
from my shoulders
as my feet hit the ground.
thinking about the summertime.
feeling sunny in my own mind.
my body is a thing to be loved.
the feeling of okayness seeping
into each of my limbs,
cushioning my joints and making
them painless.

handwritten

now that i've been
using paper to write
i don't want to write
with anything else.
i think i've become
obsessed with
how real it makes me feel
to spill my guts
in a journal i had forgotten about
so long ago.
it's almost as if i am
coming back to myself.

wet hair

after a shower,
i throw on
whatever is easiest.
whatever will encourage
me to keep smiling
even when i don't want to.

because it is all the little things
that i trudge through my memories
for.
a clean set of pajamas
after a long day
of being scared.
a lavender-vanilla scented candle
to remind me that i'm still here.

it's evenings on my floor
writing poetry.
and moments like this can be so fleeting.
they can be so easy to forget in the midst
of the chaos that is loving
everything but yourself.

dotted lines

in this journal
i write about the beach
and days with my mother
that i try to remember fondly
and without crashing into myself
and all the things she'll never be.

taking deep breaths.
reminding myself
that i am where i am now
because i forget that time has passed.
that life goes on even if
you choose not to live it.

flowers start growing and i do too

the bouquet i bought
starts opening up
in the little vase
that i've had for years.
i miss my mother
and it's a silent ache.
the wind blows away each little thing
that reminds me of her.
it is spring and maybe new things
are good.
time passes and i fit myself into
a place of acceptance of what
i couldn't change
even if i was a little bit stronger.
happiness is not a static thing.
it is fickle and fragile and
something we fight for
until our gums and knuckles
bleed.

i want to be

i want to be the kind of girl
who drinks tea
and talks about how they have learned
to accept who they are
and what they've been through.

i want to be the kind of girl
who can forgive their mother
and move on from what
she did
all those years ago.

i want to be the kind of girl
with braids in their hair
that swing from side to side
when they walk
and feel proud that i did them
all by myself.

i want to be the kind of girl
who loves to love and
doesn't mind a little heartbreak.

i want to be the kind of girl
who wakes up in the morning
and tries to continue being that girl.

i miss my mother

one day i will remember
what it meant to love my mother
and it won't sting in the ways
it does now.
i will have lived my life
and it won't matter anymore.
this is a story i tell myself
to help me fall asleep at night
when it is pouring rain
and the power flickers
and i am scared.
i miss my mother in all
the same places i did
when i was thirteen.
it never gets old
and i know it never will
but i cross my fingers
and hope that one day
the blood will just be red.

august

i walk down newbury street
and drink freshly squeezed lemonade
and squint my eyes at the taste of
a mouth full of sugar.
i get home tired from the sun.
my freckles are more
visible than ever
and my hair is a kind of bright orange
that i haven't seen on myself
since i was a kid
who cut their own bangs
with kitchen scissors
and cried when their
mother found out.
it is hard to be gentle for
a whole month,
or for many
but i remind myself
of my brother some days
and it feels like hope to remember
that i am me even after
all of this time.

sinking

i am so unlovable in the middle
of the night
when i am at my heaviest and most
tired.
there is no place to put the leftovers.
the sorry excuse of love.
i try the closets and under the bed
but i still wake up with that feeling
in my throat like i just might cry
and i think my heart has done all the sinking
it can do
until i hear your laugh in the back
of coffee shops and museums
when you've never even been
to boston.
it scares me to think about
a world where we share the same sky.
that we live in the same moments of time.

that sinking feeling

i am so sure the things i love
are always just about
to leave me.
like there is something
i need to save myself
from.
and perhaps it's my mother's
anger or my father's
absence
but when i am in my apartment alone,
i try to find a way to hurt less
and it always becomes
tangling myself up within my duvet
and saying goodnight too early
in the evening.
crying until it hurts
to see
all over something
that isn't there anymore.
loneliness never stayed
too far behind me.
it's kept up with me
and found me
a couple of times.

tulips

on my living room floor
i think about what it means
to be in love.
the raw feeling of
opening yourself up
to be scared and a mess.

the vulnerability of saying
i love you
for the first time.
kissing while wrapped within sheets
and a freshly washed duvet.
it feels like picking strawberries
hand in hand.
watching him watch you
and calling it the world.
learning to love
after losing all that you have.
as long as it's not him.

ambient lighting

i watch him
in the corner
of the room
in the yellow-warm
lighting
making out the shape of his jaw.
thinking about
cupping it
in my sorry hands.

i'm finding small moments
to love him more.
my heart yearning and fresh
with wanting.

each curve is a marvel.
something to see in awe
as he stretches
when he first wakes up
on a gloomy saturday morning.

i love him even when it rains
and nothing matters.
even when i stop believing
that i am worth
fighting for.

behind

waiting for
the perfect moment
to feel something.
anything
other than what
i am right now.

i couldn't write about
what it feels like to want to die.
there is no way to word
the slowness that comes
right before you think about
dying.

maybe it's a little bit
of everything
that i am so afraid of.
i hate the way it's keeping me
from loving the nooks and crannies
of life.
it makes me feel lonely
when everyone moves
and i watch them
know how to grow up
while i'm stagnant
and a little helpless.

i feel a nothingness when i recall my father

some days it is so easy to miss him.
it feels like a biological thing
and maybe that's because it is.
there is a hunger i call remembering.
it doesn't always hurt.
sometimes it feels like a good thing
to want to crawl into his bed
and make myself into his daughter again.
i don't bring up the memories of him,
i keep them to myself like a secret
i need to swallow.
he was not the man he should've been,
but i hold onto what could've been
as if it still matters.
as if i am still that little girl
who looks exactly like him.

it stopped hurting a while ago but i still recall it sometimes

it took me a while to get over the way you stayed / sometimes sadness looks a lot like the boy with curly hair who you loved when you were thirteen / some things should stay dead / some things should've never bloomed in the first place / i couldn't forget about it for the longest time / when i say this, i mean all of it / forgiveness looks a lot like the girl i am now / maybe there is part of me who thanks you for the marks you left / i screamed and i cried too much for my own good / my throat hurts but at least i am something else now / in a new place with someone who loves me harder / you taught me all the ways to let go / to move on from something is to kill a version of you that doesn't need to stay alive anymore / at some point you need to stop protecting yourself from something that isn't there / trudging through the gray area of you / the wounds you left on my past sting less / but i still find myself picking at the scabs sometimes / this is my way of saying i stopped loving you so long ago that i forgot what it was like to look forward to you / this is my way of saying i forgive myself now too.

writing poetry will save me in the end

i eat ice cream and call it breakfast.
i am tired by 5pm and need a nap
an hour after i wake up in the morning.
i pace my apartment in a big circle,
trying to piece together the parts of me
that ache for something more.
or just for something different.
something new.
anything that feels even remotely
like a mother's love
might fix me.
but until then i will write little lines.
things that make me feel less alone
in the midst of trying to grow up.

less than alive

there's nothing left for me to write anymore.
there's no pretty way for me to say
that i stopped feeling like i mattered so long ago
that i've become something less than alive.
to matter is to be seen.
this is the hard part.
this is where i apologize
for the chaos i am
until my tongue is sore
and it's still not enough to
redeem the way i cry when
i am alone
and beg my lover to love me
even though i know he does,
i know it.

birthdays

every year
my birthday
comes around
just the same.
i dread it each time.

swallowing the realization
that i am still
the person i was
when i was freshly sixteen.

some days i hate my own
resilience.
i wish i would let myself
give up.
and i don't fully know
what this means
but i know it's sad
because it always is.

hopeful

poetry is the thing
i run to when i am scared
or upset
or angry
and i don't know
if it's for the worst
or not
but i do know
that nothing reminds me
that i'm alive
more than writing
about tulips and
childhood.
even when it hurts
i am taken back to a place
where it doesn't
and it feels like it never will.

things

i am scared that
i will never write
a poem that i
want to read.
i am too ashamed
of my own handwriting
to stomach reading
old journal entries
and love letters to my boyfriend
from back before
we closed the distance.
it's the way i write my e's
and forget to dot my i's
that make me feel like
something ugly.
like something worth
forgetting.
because i wonder if
when i die,
my writing will live on
in anthologies and
completed poetry collections.
if i am worth that much
and you'd think that i'd know it
by heart
but truthfully
i am always worried that my words are just
ink on paper and that i am
just a vessel
in the grand scheme of things.

here's to writing poetry that makes you remember

i'm sitting in my bed
and going through poetry i wrote
when i was twenty and trying to be something.
i realize that at almost twenty-three
i am the same;
some girl needing to be saved.
some person who is wrapped up
in this idea of a perfect forever.
i listen to the cure and
try to forgive myself for the things
i needed to become so much sooner.

the biology that makes me miss my mother

i didn't just want you to love me back,
i needed it, i needed it to develop into someone
who can keep themselves alive,
because here i am, open like roadkill on a side street
and i don't know how i got here.
everything we could've been will die with me
because even at twenty i can't self regulate,
even at twenty i can't go outside.
even at twenty i yearn for my mother to tell me it's okay,
that even if the world ends tonight,
it will start up again tomorrow.
but there is no sight of the love,
i just have to hope that it'll come.

the biology that makes me miss my mother pt. 2

at eighteen i thought i'd never see you again
but more importantly, i thought that
i didn't want to.
really, it just wasn't an option,
really, a mother who flashes teeth is the same
as a father, only subtle.
but i missed my mother, and i resented it,
i thought it made me weak, i thought it meant
that she won.
it took me years to admit what it was doing to me,
that i was crying in my sleep and
reaching for my phone hoping she tried to call.
i still make space for her, and i probably always will,
even at my limited capacity.
but she doesn't take me up on it,
and this means that i am not only motherless,
but that i might die in the end
and even if i wanted to live, i wouldn't have
the choice.

here is where i go if i had never taken the time to love you

i see lights, i see big buildings that are bigger than even my childhood dreams. i can look out my apartment window and plan all the ways i will leave it. there is the smell of fresh pastries on the way to the local bookshop where i like to write, and for the first time, i notice it. for the first time i take a step back and sync my breath with the fall of my foot. the snow is finally starting to line the windows and it's my favorite part. i sit down after ordering all on my own, after talking through the lump of cotton in my throat. i write my heart out, i write about what matters, and not one page is lined with you. here, i like coffee. here, i try new things. i don't reject possibility and cry under the covers over the uncertainty. ease is plastered on everyone's face, over mine and we collectively do not think of you. i walk home and its near dark. i pass a bench, i pass a park. this is me without my eyes glued to the ground, or completely shut. i unlock my apartment door and i don't check it twice. my clothes drop off my body and silk linens hold me hostage in a sweet way. i play jazz on my record player and slow dance in the mirror because i'm not worried, because there was no last call, or left over anger. where we end up becomes meaningless.

summer daydreams

when i think about family,
i think about the kids i will have.
the sweetness of a lover
who loves my voids and eats me whole,
black seeds and all.
the pain is folded neatly
in the cupboard and has been for a while now.
i only grieve my parents
on the really bad days—
the ones where the pancakes burn and i'm out
of batter before i'm able to try again.
in the quiet, after the kids are on the bus,
my lover kisses my cheek before heading off
into the world.
i sit myself on the porch to write
and it's not because of my mother's creativity
or my father's absence.
i write and it doesn't hurt
and it hasn't in a while.

daughters ache

it didn't matter
how hurt i was,
the world needed me,
weak or not.
i was important.
i was big and mighty and nine
and to me it was love,
i didn't know it could be anything
but love.

amnesia

i didn't mean to be catastrophic,
at least not for this long,
but my mother, oh, my mother—
i still sit on the bathroom floor
in the middle of the night
like i am still that child
with something to be scared of.
i tell her the life i've lived is not normal,
that it's grimy and i refuse to
pass it down to my children
the way she did
and maybe it was payback for the childhood
she didn't get either
but i still feel the burning,
years later,
and the fire never really settles,
because you don't forget
motherhood and starvation,
not at fifteen.
even though i know she will
always be counting on it.

invisible man

i never wanted him to think about me,
about my softness, all the things that
make me lovable, or at least, approachable.
about my weakness, the shaking and
the begging, like i was dying
and maybe i always almost was,
because the satisfaction,
it made him that much hungrier, that much bigger
and it confused me.
but i wanted him to know
what he did without me having
to admit that i loved him
because that is my guilt
all on its own.

inauthenticity

i meet myself in the yellow light
of the bathroom mirror
with overgrown sideburns and no sense of self.
i think about the emptiness, the voids
between voids
and how only five percent of the ocean
has been explored.
i put on a chapped lipped smile
and tell myself that all the stolen strings
holding me together feel like home,
that it could feel like me if i just
tried a little harder.
if i
just stopped picking at the scabs
and let the end of me and the beginning
of everyone else become
seamless.

borderline

sometimes i have these moments
where my shoes tie themselves
and i'm ready to run.
where my lungs never need to rest
and i never have to look back.
as if i could 180 my life, maybe even save myself
just a little
and i don't feel an ounce of fear.
there is no worry of if i'll get there,
i just believe that i will arrive.
but it's always so sporadic, so inevitably
going to abandon me by the time my shoes
are on the right feet.
it feels like a vulgar kind of chaos,
a mania level happiness.
it's like kicking your arms and legs when your head
has been under for too long.
my feet never touch the ground
and hope leaves before i'm able
to make it mine.

personality

there are so many different versions of me
that want different things
and there's not enough time in one life, in one body
to give each of them what they want
so there's a lot of picking,
a lot of neglecting and ignoring.
i haven't quite decided which i want to be yet
and maybe i never will and i'll fight
my own existence forever
but i hope one day that i settle and know
and i hope that they let me.

thank you

don't tell me the stars make you think of me.
i know i'm bloodier than that, more vulgar than
even their version of dying.
see me as i am and then take it too.
to your bed, turn it into ours
unfold me and then try putting me back together.
i'm not angry, it's just hot in here and
i don't know how to tell the story.
partly because i don't remember.
partly because nothing really matters
but my head on the pillow and your hands
on my chest.
this is what the movies were talking about.
the things my mother never wanted for herself.
i got the softness,
the tender heart with heavy fists on rainy days.
i understand i say, it's not easy to love me but you do.

out of body

crying in the shower, relentless and
almost bloody,
yours or mine, i ask
and there's no answer.
i love you, you say
and i have nothing left to add.
i look to you and there's not nothing,
a void with a dream, i call you, i call myself, really.
i was never good at this part,
the loving, or mostly the staying.
break the mirror, eat the glass
and swallow your insecurity.
pick up the phone and call him,
tell him what you've done, that you've told
what he's done.
this is what it takes to realize
you couldn't be less in love
with the idea of yourself and
this isn't even the sickest part.
there's still a father, now let's not tell stories
but this one hurt.
on the tile floor, quenching your thirst,
looking for something deep in the caverns
of your abandoned heart
yours or mine, i ask,
ours.

mess in the kitchen

is there a place between your ribs that i live?
somewhere you don't tell the ones after me about?
i write and catch myself stopping to wonder
if you'll read any of it and be proud of me.
it was always exciting to you
or maybe you just loved me and it looked
like happiness.
though i was so disappointed back then;
i've never told the story of your disappearing and
me thinking you loved her more than me.
i don't want to say you're a lover
because you're angrier than that
but there were moments i could've sung
forever, moments i could've stayed
forever.

weekends

the feeling of the sheets as i wrap myself up
and curl into something so small and unimportant
that nothing hurts anymore.
sundays are for getting better
and maybe i will let it be my turn this time.
i'll stay in bed and read poetry i love,
kiss my boyfriend and even though the blinds
will open and the anxiety will be waiting for me,
i'm not hurting, and i forget
what it feels like
for a little while.

emergency services

it starts with a bridge. google maps says it's twenty minutes by bike and i don't remember if i know how to ride but i'm desperate. i don't know what to do with myself, i just know i need to do something before i do other things. by the beach, the air is cooler and it's not like it's unbearable but i wish i could remember something warm. the moon is just about full, the waves are calm and i'm trying to figure out how to be. this is a big thought, big feelings that i don't think i have the body for. mondays come around and they bring clock work with them. i think of the er, even start heading there. i circle back to the bridge. there's so many chances but not enough of them are mine. i'm afraid of heights but it couldn't matter less right now. i could step forward and it would be so easy. i could go back home and it would be so hard. tell me about surviving and how it's worth it. is there really a light that will make up for all this lost time? i can't believe it's 5am and i'm still nothing. i know a lot about bleeding, how long it lasts and i've got the color down to a hex code. this is not supposed to be a talent but maybe it should be, maybe because i haven't lost too much of it yet. i hop off my bike just to hop back on. this is supposed to be the end, but i never catch a break. there's too much time for me to try even though i don't want to. i run over rocks on the way home, almost fall and this doesn't scare me when my life was at stake. what scares me is people not knowing, not understanding what i mean when i say i'm not built to be a person. i'm on the way home and then i'm there. i make it out alive but do i really because head on the pillow, there's always going to be a bridge.

emergency services part two

i call my case manager from the emergency line
and tell her i can't handle the process of getting better.
she insists i try and i insist that i have, so many times.
this wasn't supposed to make me cry but it does, these things always do.
tomorrow i will spend eight hours talking about
where it hurts, how much it burns when i'm alone.
i'm not ready to let people in, or maybe it's about
letting the pain out.
who am i without it? what if it has become the structure
of everything i am and can be? what if i don't have shape
without something so hard holding me in place?
i ask my mom to ease me. i call four times throughout the day
and i don't hear back.
my boyfriend's mother tells me she's proud of me,
tells me i'm brave, tells me i'm strong.
oh, the things i could've become had my mother
loved me back.
these are things i think about in the shower, when i'm trying to find
some peace of mind, but end up halfway
down the drain and just barely okay enough
with my sadness to stand back up.
time passes faster than i realize
and i am almost twenty,
i have my own health insurance and even
make my own doctor's appointments.
i thought by now, it would
be better, that i would feel better, but now i swear
my medication isn't working and i cry
until i can't cry anymore.

first love

it's a mountain to climb, quite a story to tell.
i don't want to be cliche but it was.
maybe it was almost forever, maybe it should've been
but i try to be okay with the fact that it's not. the
yearning in my heart makes a victim out of me. i
watch movies to reminisce without opening the
door of the messy concept we made out of love.
i hope there's more to life than missing you. it comes
in these waves that i would say break my heart
like nothing else has, but the way you left
had me in bed crying to songs i sung to you
when all you wanted was to fall asleep.
sometimes i still wish i had picked up. sometimes
i still wish you had showed up. when you watched me,
you saw me and i wish i could stop writing about you
but i've never been looked at like that before.

the buzzing of a streetlight reminds me of the sounds of someone i once knew

i lived in a small town, somewhere everyone knows everyone, and i knew you. i knew the things you wanted to shed, how you fit in the front seat of your car and that even though i hated the way the inside smelled, it always meant i was with you. i remember this while walking to the gas station on the corner, it's been so long since summers in the park were our thing. late nights made me hate the sun, the laughter over the phone, you falling asleep at your desk just to be near me a little bit longer. that made it love. i think we made it love and then we didn't know what to do with it. days in the sun where you made me feel like i could be the most beautiful woman you've ever met and me, so scared, so uncertain of what it meant to want you in the ways i did. i couldn't piece us together, i knew this was going to hurt. i knew before i didn't pick up your last phone call, that i'd hate you and hate you and hate you until i missed you.

for old times sake

the emptiness that is a sunday morning,
you will not admit that you're heartbroken,
not yet, only because that will mean you'll have to talk about the man
who did this to you, and that's not even the hardest part of missing
someone. it's not only that he stopped loving you, but that he stopped
thinking about you in a way that was once everything. you can't play
the beautiful woman because he doesn't look in your direction any-
more. his strings are not yours to pull, and his weak spot doesn't look
like you and you aren't sure when it became something else, you just
know you aren't his. you don't get your way, not here. you get these
sunday mornings, empty and quiet but damning you to hell. in another
life his promise is not only kept but it's yours.

some things you can't take back

i think about the weeds growing
through my ribs and the vines
weaving around my fingers.
i'm left with a ledge
that seems to only send me back up.
there's nothing here
and my war of a life
seems to have hit a dead end.
i never thought
i'd mourn my own death
but i do.

survival of the fittest

i know i can't ask
a bear to spare me
just because
he loved me once
but he loved me
once.

stained glass

i put my two left feet on his spine
and become his jewelry box ballerina.
i dance and trip into his orbit and it's home.
in the light, in the dark, it's all the same.
i see stars and it's just him.
he's so bright with every sharp edge;
like a knife, like a rebirth
and i consume him, not slowly, but all at once.
there's no rain but his voice is a kind of cleanse
that makes you believe in purity;
he showed me what it means to believe in god
and i swear it's always been him.
he's holy, and he knows that
but he's a martyr sometimes, for me, anyway.
i'm sleeping in the light because the night
never does come around when he does.
he's suffocation and a deep breath all in one
it's passion between chaos and it's beautifully real like this.
it's miles without parting, without breaks, without ever
being anything but one.
it doesn't get more captivating than him
not in this eon, at least.

mine

i want to
explore a new city, fall in love with
empty spaces and buy myself a hot chocolate
to watch the snow with.
i'm alone, but not sad, not really anything at all.
 just being
and without the means
to buy the world, i'll still say i'm satisfied.

i have the dream of sleeping next to
a small window in an apartment
close enough to feel the vibrations
of the train coming and going.
to wrap up into myself and kiss the day goodbye,
with nothing left over but the silence
and myself.

true love and coffee mugs

i want to know what
your loneliness looks like.
if it sits idle at the coffee shop
with you,
watching and hovering close enough
to stir your spoon.
or if it waits until the quiet sinks in
along with the darkness and steps out
when the moon does.
does it settle in your chest
or pounce on your shoulders?
is it a lump in your throat with a knife
to your back or a safe place,
almost like home?
and if i asked,
would you let me see it?
and would you let me stay
even after i have?

tx

he drives me around his neighborhood
and doesn't once remind me of my father
on the busy road.
i think maybe i could go deeper than
just surviving,
i think maybe i could live without
the heaviness
and i do
i do.
and i laugh loud
and real
on the way to pick up dinner.
i stick my head out the window
like a dog catching sunlight;
i don't want to go home.

road trip

so, as it turns out
the moon is not following
my car
and she does not metaphorically
hold my hand the rest of the way home
and all along avoiding
the emptiness, the trench
in my stomach
that does not cease,
all the while wanting,
always wanting.

slipping through her fingers

i love my mother, i do, and i wish we
could be adults about it more often
but she doesn't always pick up
and no matter what, in any life,
i don't think she'd ever be able
to love me if she doesn't love herself.
one day i'm going to be forty and want my mother
to scoop me up and hold me when i'm depressed
and i know this because it has already started to happen
despite her never knowing me before.
i am lifelessly waiting for something
that i'm not sure will ever come
and it's not like it's hope,
it's less intentional, almost like it's the last option
and sometimes i really believe it is
and i don't know what it is that will
soothe me in the meantime.
i just know i need somewhere
to let the stuck parts of me
sink into nothing.

trails

the trees still wet,
i carry my weight to work.
i ask for more peace, just a little,
and i don't think i've gotten it yet.
either that or it just isn't enough
because i can get greedy when it comes
to feeling happy
but this is just because i haven't had it much
and that should be fair.
see my cries as desperation because
i'm trying to be more transparent.
i would simply like to live
and do nothing more.
no longer fight my existence, or suffer
under the waves of the grief
i keep reminding myself of.
i think i am the only one
still this far behind,
struggling to get ahead
but i'm trying,
i know i'm crying but i swear
i'm still trying.

afterword

it is brave of us to sit here and read poetry when we could be doing other things. worse things. i've been writing since i was twelve with the hope that maybe one day i'd grow up and be doing exactly what i'm doing right now; laying down, messy headed and writing something that will make someone feel something. it's not easy to grow up yet we do. and we do it every day. we age and we slowly take a different shape in the passage of time and it's brave of us to admit that. poetry is not meant to fix everything, but it gets pretty close every time i sit down to write about missing my mother and hating our estrangement. or when i write about summers in cape may spent with my extended family.

i miss my long hair and it's so easy to write about the things that hurt. i usually find myself trying to fix my broken heart by reminding myself that i am not the only one that falls apart. i have been weak and i will be weak again. how human of us to be sad sometimes. i hope you know that in the depths of our humanity, the dirty and sticky thing we call living, you are something that has the potential to become more at any time. being important is something i grew up wanting. craving. i thought that i needed to be seen by other people in order to consider myself alive. to consider myself worth something. but even in my aloneness, and in yours, we are everything we have been and want to be simultaneously. we will ebb and flow. wax and wane. we will cry and scream and kick our feet just as much as we will laugh and smile and feel free.

about the author

Gracie Drew (they/she/he) is a trans and disabled poet and romance writer who lives in Boston, MA with their partner and service dog. They enjoy writing about trauma, mental health and the healing journey of someone with trauma and bipolar disorder.

When they aren't writing, they're reading the latest poetry and romance and growing their never ending tbr.

Instagram: @poetgracie